cooking
for two

THE AUSTRALIAN
Women's Weekly

CONTENTS

AUSTRALIAN CUP AND
SPOON MEASUREMENTS
ARE METRIC.
A CONVERSION CHART
APPEARS ON PAGE 77.

· ·

There's something wonderful about a quiet,
intimate dinner for two. Whether you're
cooking for a partner, a child or a housemate,
these recipes are fuss-free and save you from
the nightmare of too many leftovers – all you
need is someone special to share them with.
And what better way to end a meal for two
than with a banana split?

Pamela Clark

Food Director

THAI BEEF SALAD WITH CHILLI, GARLIC AND LIME

prep + cook time 30 minutes **serves** 2
nutritional count per serving 8.3g total fat
(3.2g saturated fat); 1133kJ (271 cal);
18.6g carbohydrate; 29.5g protein; 1.5g fibre

250g (8 ounces) beef eye fillet, trimmed
60g (2 ounces) rice vermicelli
½ lebanese cucumber (65g), seeded,
   sliced thinly
¼ cup firmly packed fresh coriander
   (cilantro) leaves
2 tablespoons fresh thai basil leaves
5cm (2 inch) stick lemon grass (10g),
   crushed, sliced thinly
1 fresh kaffir lime leaf, shredded finely
1 shallot (25g), sliced thinly
1 tablespoon fried shallots

thai dressing
1 fresh small red thai (serrano) chilli, halved
1 small clove garlic, quartered
¼ teaspoon caster (superfine) sugar
2 tablespoons lime juice
1 tablespoon fish sauce

1 Cook beef on heated oiled grill plate
(or grill or barbecue) until cooked as desired.
Cover beef; stand 5 minutes then slice thinly.
2 Meanwhile, place vermicelli in medium
heatproof bowl, cover with boiling water;
stand until tender, drain. Rinse under cold
water; drain.
3 Make thai dressing.
4 Combine beef, vermicelli, cucumber, herbs,
lemon grass, lime leaf and sliced shallot
in large bowl. Divide salad among serving
plates; drizzle with dressing, sprinkle with
fried shallots.
thai dressing Using mortar and pestle, crush
chilli, garlic and sugar to a paste. Combine
paste with remaining ingredients in small bowl.
tip Fried shallots can be bought in jars from Asian
grocery stores.

SALADS

couscous salad with haloumi

COUSCOUS SALAD WITH HALOUMI

prep + cook time 20 minutes serves 2
nutritional count per serving 45.4g total fat
(16.4g saturated fat); 3641kJ (871 cal);
73g carbohydrate; 46.6g protein; 4.6g fibre

¾ cup (150g) couscous
¾ cup (180ml) boiling water
1½ tablespoons lemon juice
1½ tablespoons olive oil
½ teaspoon ground cumin
¼ cup (35g) coarsely chopped dried dates
¼ cup (35g) roasted slivered almonds
⅓ cup coarsely chopped fresh mint
250g (8 ounce) packet haloumi cheese,
    sliced thickly

1 Combine couscous with the water in
medium heatproof bowl, cover; stand about
5 minutes or until liquid is absorbed, fluffing
with fork occasionally.
2 Combine juice, oil and cumin in screw-top
jar; shake well.
3 Add cumin dressing, dates, nuts and mint to
couscous; mix gently.
4 Heat oiled large frying pan; cook cheese until
browned both sides. Top salad with cheese.

CREAMY CHICKEN AND PASTA SALAD

prep + cook time 35 minutes serves 2
nutritional count per serving 39.1g total fat
(8.8g saturated fat); 3097kJ (741 cal);
67.5g carbohydrate; 27.1g protein; 5.7g fibre

1½ cups (375ml) water
200g (6½ ounces) chicken breast fillets
250g (8 ounces) large pasta shells
1 celery stalk (150g), trimmed, sliced thinly
1 small red onion (100g), sliced thinly
½ cup (60g) roasted pecans
¼ cup (45g) thinly sliced dill pickles
30g (1 ounce) baby rocket (arugula) leaves
creamy tarragon dressing
⅓ cup (100g) mayonnaise
¼ cup (60g) sour cream
1 tablespoon lemon juice
2 teaspoons finely chopped fresh tarragon

1 Bring the water to the boil in small
saucepan, add chicken; simmer, covered,
about 10 minutes. Cool chicken in poaching
liquid 10 minutes; drain, slice thinly.
2 Meanwhile, cook pasta in large saucepan of
boiling water until tender; drain. Rinse under
cold water; drain.
3 Make creamy tarragon dressing.
4 Combine pasta in large bowl with chicken,
dressing and remaining ingredients.
creamy tarragon dressing Combine
ingredients in small bowl.

tip Cornichon, French for gherkin, is a very small
variety of pickled cucumber; it can be used in place
of the dill pickles.

creamy chicken and pasta salad

POACHED TROUT AND POTATO SALAD

prep + cook time **25 minutes** serves 2
nutritional count per serving **24.3g total fat**
(3.9g saturated fat); 2031kJ (486 cal);
29.3g carbohydrate; 34.9g protein; 5.1g fibre

400g (12½ ounces) kipfler potatoes,
    unpeeled, halved
2 cups (500ml) water
2 x 5cm (2 inch) strips lemon rind
1 sprig fresh dill
300g (9½ ounces) ocean trout fillets
½ small red onion (50g), sliced thinly
½ lebanese cucumber (65g), seeded,
    sliced thinly
30g (1 ounce) rocket (arugula) leaves
lemon and dill dressing
2 tablespoons olive oil
1½ tablespoons lemon juice
1 small clove garlic, crushed
2 teaspoons finely chopped fresh dill
2 teaspoons rinsed, drained baby capers

1 Boil, steam or microwave potato until
tender; drain.
2 Combine the water, rind and dill in medium
saucepan; bring to the boil. Add fish; simmer,
covered, about 10 minutes or until cooked as
desired. Drain fish; discard cooking liquid.
Flake fish coarsely into large bowl; discard skin.
3 Meanwhile, make lemon and dill dressing.
4 Add potato, dressing and remaining
ingredients to bowl with fish; toss gently
to combine.
lemon and dill dressing Combine
ingredients in screw-top jar; shake well.
tip Poaching is a great low-fat way to cook fish
because you don't need to use oil. You'll have very
tender flesh, lightly infused with the flavours of the
poaching liquid. Ensure the liquid is only just simmering,
as slow cooking provides the most delicate flesh.

peppered lamb with watercress, pea and mint salad

PEPPERED LAMB WITH WATERCRESS, PEA AND MINT SALAD

prep + cook time **30 minutes** serves 2
nutritional count per serving **31.1g total fat**
(12g saturated fat); 2006kJ (480 cal);
5.1g carbohydrate; 43.2g protein; 5g fibre

1 tablespoon mixed peppercorns
1 tablespoon olive oil
300g (9½ ounces) lamb fillets
½ cup (80g) fresh or frozen peas
125g (4 ounces) yellow teardrop
    tomatoes, halved
60g (2 ounces) firmly packed
    trimmed watercress
200g (6½ ounces) fetta cheese,
    cut into thin strips
2 tablespoons coarsely chopped
    fresh mint
white wine vinaigrette
1½ tablespoons white wine vinegar
2 teaspoons olive oil

1 Using mortar and pestle, crush peppercorns until ground coarsely. Combine ground peppercorns, oil and lamb in medium bowl. Cook lamb in heated oiled medium frying pan until cooked as desired. Cover lamb; stand 5 minutes then slice thinly.
2 Meanwhile, make white wine vinaigrette.
3 Boil, steam or microwave peas until tender; drain. Rinse under cold water; drain.
4 Combine lamb, peas, vinaigrette and remaining ingredients in large bowl.
white wine vinaigrette Combine ingredients in screw-top jar; shake well.

BARBECUED PORK AND CRUNCHY NOODLE SALAD

prep time **20 minutes** serves 2
nutritional count per serving **29.7g total fat**
(7.6g saturated fat); 1789kJ (428 cal);
17.6g carbohydrate; 20.4g protein; 6.1g fibre

3 trimmed red radishes (50g), sliced thinly,
    cut into matchsticks
1 small red capsicum (bell pepper)
    (150g) sliced thinly
1 baby buk choy (150g), sliced thinly
2 green onions (scallions), sliced thinly
⅓ cup (25g) bean sprouts
2 tablespoons roasted slivered almonds
100g (3 ounce) packet fried noodles
150g (4½ ounces) chinese barbecued pork,
    sliced thinly
sweet-sour dressing
1 tablespoon peanut oil
1 tablespoon white vinegar
1 tablespoon light brown sugar
1 tablespoons light soy sauce
½ teaspoon sesame oil
1 clove garlic, crushed

1 Combine ingredients for sweet-sour dressing in screw-top jar; shake well.
2 Combine salad ingredients in large bowl with dressing.

barbecued pork and crunchy noodle salad

egg and bacon salad

EGG AND BACON SALAD

prep + cook time **25 minutes** serves **2**
nutritional count per serving **29.2g total fat**
(6.9g saturated fat); 1965kJ (470 cal);
25.9g carbohydrate; 25g protein; 2.6g fibre

**1 small kumara (orange sweet potato)
(250g), cut into 2.5cm (1 inch) pieces
cooking-oil spray
2 rindless bacon slices (130g)
3 hard-boiled eggs, quartered
½ stalk celery (75g), trimmed, sliced thinly
40g (1½ ounces) mesclun**
honey mustard dressing
**¼ cup (75g) mayonnaise
1½ tablespoons cider vinegar
2 teaspoons honey
1 teaspoon wholegrain mustard**

1 Preheat oven to 220°C/425°F.
2 Place kumara on oven tray; spray with
cooking oil. Roast, uncovered, about
20 minutes or until tender.
3 Meanwhile, cook bacon in heated medium
frying pan; drain on absorbent paper.
Chop coarsely.
4 Make honey mustard dressing.
5 Combine kumara, bacon, dressing and
remaining ingredients in large bowl.
honey mustard dressing Combine
ingredients in small bowl.

prawn, crab and avocado salad

PRAWN, CRAB AND AVOCADO SALAD

prep + cook time **25 minutes** serves **2**
nutritional count per serving **26.5g total fat**
(4.4g saturated fat); 1718kJ (411 cal);
11.5g carbohydrate; 30.7g protein; 2.8g fibre

**8 cooked medium king prawns (shrimp) (400g)
2 large butter (boston) lettuce leaves
125g (4 ounces) crab meat, shredded coarsely
½ large avocado (160g), sliced thinly**
thousand island dressing
**¼ cup (75g) mayonnaise
2 teaspoons tomato sauce (ketchup)
¼ small red capsicum (bell pepper) (35g),
chopped finely
¼ small white onion (20g), grated finely
4 pimiento-stuffed green olives, chopped
1 teaspoon lemon juice**

1 Make thousand island dressing.
2 Shell and devein prawns, leaving tails intact.
3 Divide lettuce leaves among serving plates;
divide prawns, crab and avocado among
lettuce leaves. Drizzle with dressing.
thousand island dressing Combine
ingredients in small bowl.

BEEF WITH ASPARAGUS
AND OYSTER SAUCE

prep + cook time 25 min **serves** 2
nutritional count per serving 15.1g total fat
(3.8g saturated fat); 1166kJ (279 cal);
6.1g carbohydrate; 28.6g protein; 2g fibre

1 tablespoon peanut oil
250g (8 ounces) beef rump steak, sliced thinly
1 small brown onion (80g), cut into wedges
170g asparagus, trimmed,
     cut into 2.5cm (1 inch) lengths
1 clove garlic, chopped finely
1 tablespoon oyster sauce
2 teaspoons japanese soy sauce

1 Heat half the oil in wok; stir-fry beef, in
batches, until browned.
2 Heat remaining oil in wok; stir-fry onion until
softened. Add asparagus; stir-fry until tender.
Return beef to wok with garlic; stir-fry until
fragrant. Add sauces; stir-fry until hot, season
to taste. For extra heat, sprinkle with sliced
fresh red chilli.

tips Try broccolini or broccoli instead of the asparagus.
Serve with steamed jasmine rice.

STIR-FRIES

PAD THAI

prep + cook time **30 minutes** serves **2**
nutritional count per serving **19.6g total fat**
(3.4g saturated fat); 1246kJ (298 cal);
15.1g carbohydrate; 13.4g protein; 4.3g fibre

100g (3 ounces) dried rice stick noodles
1 clove garlic, quartered
1 fresh small red thai (serrano) chilli,
  chopped coarsely
1 tablespoon peanut oil
1 egg, beaten lightly
½ cup (40g) fried shallots
½ x 125g (4 ounce) packet fried tofu,
  cut into 2.5cm (1 inch) cubes
1½ tablespoons roasted unsalted peanuts,
  chopped coarsely
1½ cups (180g) bean sprouts
3 green onions (scallions), sliced thinly
1 tablespoon light soy sauce
2 teaspoons lime juice
1 tablespoon coarsely chopped
  fresh coriander (cilantro)

1 Place noodles in medium heatproof bowl, cover with boiling water; stand until just tender, drain.
2 Meanwhile, using mortar and pestle, crush garlic and chilli to a paste.
3 Heat remaining oil in wok. Pour egg into wok; cook over medium heat, tilting pan, until almost set. Remove omelette from wok; roll tightly, slice thinly.
4 Heat remaining oil in wok, stir-fry garlic paste and shallots until fragrant. Add tofu; stir-fry 1 minute. Add half the nuts, half the sprouts and half the onion; stir-fry until spouts are just wilted.
5 Add noodles, sauce and juice; stir-fry until hot. Remove from heat; sprinkle omelette, coriander and remaining nuts, sprouts and onion over pad thai.

mongolian lamb

MONGOLIAN LAMB

prep + cook time **25 minutes** serves **2**
nutritional count per serving **16.5g total fat**
(3.7g saturated fat); 1459kJ (349 cal);
15.4g carbohydrate; 31.4g protein; 4g fibre

125g (4 ounces) lamb fillet, sliced thinly
1 teaspoon light soy sauce
1 teaspoon cornflour (cornstarch)
1cm (½ inch) piece fresh ginger (5g), grated
1 small clove garlic, crushed
2 teaspoons mirin
½ teaspoon sesame oil
1 tablespoon peanut oil
1 small brown onion (80g), cut into wedges
1 small red capsicum (bell pepper) (150g),
    sliced thinly
2 teaspoons hoisin sauce
2 teaspoons oyster sauce
2 teaspoons water
60g (2 ounces) snow peas, trimmed
½ fresh long red chilli, chopped finely
1 green onion (scallion), sliced thinly

1 Combine lamb, soy sauce, cornflour, ginger,
garlic, mirin and sesame oil in small bowl.
2 Heat half the peanut oil in wok; stir-fry lamb
mixture until browned. Remove from wok.
3 Heat remaining oil in wok; stir-fry brown
onion and capsicum until tender. Return lamb
to wok with sauces, the water and peas; stir-fry
until hot. Remove from heat; stir in chilli and
half the green onion. Serve sprinkled with
remaining green onion.

tips **Serve with steamed jasmine rice or noodles.**
Lamb mixture can be marinated for 3 hours or
overnight in the fridge.

tofu, cashew and vegetable stir-fry

TOFU, CASHEW AND VEGETABLE
STIR-FRY

prep + cook time **15 minutes** serves **2**
nutritional count per serving **22.6g total fat**
(3.4g saturated fat); 1563kJ (374 cal);
20.9g carbohydrate; 18.2g protein; 8.4g fibre

1 tablespoon vegetable oil
½ fresh long red chilli, sliced thinly
250g (8 ounces) packaged fresh
    stir-fry vegetables
200g (6½ ounces) packaged marinated
    tofu pieces, chopped coarsely
¼ cup (40g) roasted unsalted cashews
2 tablespoons hoisin sauce
2 teaspoons lime juice

1 Heat oil in wok; stir-fry chilli, vegetables, tofu
and nuts until vegetables are just tender.
2 Add sauce and juice; stir-fry until hot.

five-spiced chicken and noodles

1 Cook noodles in small saucepan of boiling water until tender; drain.

2 Combine chicken, cornflour and five-spice in medium bowl. Heat half the oil in wok; stir-fry chicken, in batches, until browned. Remove from wok.

3 Heat remaining oil in wok; stir-fry capsicum, garlic and ginger until capsicum is tender. Return chicken to wok with noodles, sprouts, onion, sauces and the water; stir-fry until hot, season to taste.

SANG CHOY BOW

prep + cook time **30 minutes** serves **2**
nutritional count per serving **11.5g total fat**
(3.6g saturated fat); 1112kJ (266 cal);
8.9g carbohydrate; 29.3g protein; 4.1g fibre

2 teaspoons sesame oil
1 small brown onion (80g), chopped finely
1 clove garlic, crushed
1cm (½ inch) piece fresh ginger (5g), grated
250g (8 ounces) minced (ground) pork
1 tablespoon water
60g (2 ounces) shiitake mushrooms, chopped finely
1 tablespoon light soy sauce
1 tablespoon oyster sauce
2 teaspoons lime juice
1 cup (80g) bean sprouts, trimmed
2 green onions (scallions), sliced thinly
2 tablespoons coarsely chopped fresh coriander (cilantro)
6 large butter (boston) lettuce leaves

1 Heat oil in wok; stir-fry brown onion, garlic and ginger until onion softens. Add pork; stir-fry until changed in colour.

2 Add the water, mushrooms, sauces and juice; stir-fry until mushrooms are tender. Remove from heat. Add sprouts, green onion and coriander; toss to combine.

3 Spoon sang choy bow into lettuce leaves to serve.

FIVE-SPICED CHICKEN AND NOODLES

prep + cook time **35 minutes** serves **2**
nutritional count per serving **12.9g total fat**
(2.7g saturated fat); 2153kJ (515 cal);
53g carbohydrate; 43.6g protein; 3.6g fibre

125g (4 ounces) dried thin egg noodles
300g (9½ ounces) chicken breast fillets, sliced thinly
1 tablespoon cornflour (cornstarch)
½ teaspoon five-spice powder
1 tablespoon peanut oil
1 small red capsicum (bell pepper) (150g), sliced thinly
1 clove garlic, crushed
2.5cm (1 inch) piece fresh ginger (15g), grated
½ cup (40g) bean sprouts
2 green onions (scallions), sliced thinly
1 tablespoon dark soy sauce
1 tablespoon sweet chilli sauce
1 tablespoon water

sang choy bow

swordfish and scallops

SWORDFISH AND SCALLOPS

prep + cook time 30 minutes serves 2
nutritional count per serving 12.3g total fat
(2.5g saturated fat); 1258kJ (301 cal); 15.6g
carbohydrate; 29.7g protein; 4.6g fibre

1 tablespoon peanut oil
200g (6½ ounces) swordfish steak,
    cut into strips
150g (4½ ounces) scallops, without roe
1 clove garlic, crushed
2.5cm (1 inch) piece fresh ginger (10g), grated
1 medium carrot (120g), cut into matchsticks
1 shallot (25g), sliced thinly
½ x 227g (7 ounce) can water chestnuts,
    rinsed, halved
1 small red capsicum (bell pepper) (150g),
    sliced thinly
1 tablespoon water
2 teaspoons oyster sauce
2 teaspoons light soy sauce
2 teaspoons sweet chilli sauce
1 teaspoon golden syrup or treacle
75g (2½ ounces) snow peas,
    trimmed, sliced diagonally

1 Heat half the oil in wok; stir-fry swordfish
until browned. Remove from wok.
2 Add scallops, garlic and ginger to wok;
stir-fry until scallops change in colour.
Remove from wok.
3 Heat remaining oil in wok; stir-fry carrot
and shallot until browned. Add chestnuts,
capsicum, the water, sauces and syrup;
stir-fry until mixture thickens slightly.
4 Return seafood to wok with snow peas;
stir-fry until just tender.

BEEF KWAY TEO

prep + cook time 20 minutes serves 2
nutritional count per serving 21.8g total fat
(6.8g saturated fat); 2362kJ (565 cal);
54.2g carbohydrate; 33.7g protein; 3.6g fibre

1½ tablespoons oyster sauce
1 tablespoon kecap manis
1 tablespoon chinese cooking wine
½ teaspoon sambal oelek
1 clove garlic, crushed

beef kway teo

1cm (½ inch) piece fresh ginger (5g), grated
1 tablespoon peanut oil
250g (8 ounces) beef strips
½ x 450g (14½ ounce) packet fresh
    wide rice noodles
2 green onions (scallions),
    cut into 2.5cm (1 inch) lengths
1 small red capsicum (bell pepper)
    (150g), sliced thinly
1 tablespoon coarsely chopped garlic chives
1 cup (80g) bean sprouts

1 Combine sauce, kecap manis, cooking
wine, sambal, garlic and ginger in small jug.
2 Heat half the oil in wok; stir-fry beef, in
batches, until browned.
3 Meanwhile, place noodles in medium
heatproof bowl, cover with boiling water;
separate with fork, drain.
4 Heat remaining oil in wok; stir-fry onion
and capsicum until capsicum is tender.
5 Return beef to wok with sauce mixture,
noodles, chives and sprouts; stir-fry until hot.
tip Garlic chives have rougher, flatter leaves than
simple chives, and possess a pink-tinged teardrop-
shaped flowering bud at the end. They can be used as
a salad green, or steamed and eaten as a vegetable.

PIZZA MEXICANA

prep + cook time **20 minutes** serves **2**
nutritional count per serving **9.5g total fat**
(4.7g saturated fat); 1689kJ (404 cal);
54.7g carbohydrate; 21g protein; 6.6g fibre

Preheat oven to 180°C/350°F. Place 2 pocket
pitta breads (170g) on oven tray. Spread with
½ cup canned refried beans; top with ½ finely
chopped small red capsicum (bell pepper),
1 tablespoon sweet chilli sauce and ⅓ cup
pizza cheese. Cook about 15 minutes or until
cheese melts. Sprinkle 2 thinly sliced green
onions (scallions) over pizza just before serving.

TURKEY ON TOASTED TURKISH

prep + cook time **10 minutes** serves **2**
nutritional count per serving **7g total fat**
(2.2g saturated fat); 1659kJ (397 cal);
58.5g carbohydrate; 22.4g protein; 3.1g fibre

Split 2 small turkish bread rolls in half.
Spread 2 tablespoons cranberry sauce onto
cut sides then sandwich 60g (2 ounces)
shaved turkey, 30g (1 ounce) shaved
reduced-fat swiss cheese and 30g (1 ounce)
baby spinach leaves between pieces.
Toast in sandwich press until golden brown.

COPPA AND RICOTTA PANINI

prep + cook time **20 minutes** serves **2**
nutritional count per serving **18.2g total fat**
(6.7g saturated fat); 2036kJ (487 cal);
51.3g carbohydrate; 27.6g protein; 3g fibre

Halve 2 small focaccia rolls. Combine
2 tablespoons black olive tapenade and
1 tablespoon balsamic vinegar in small bowl;
spread over bottom half of each roll.
Combine 125g (4 ounces) ricotta cheese with
¼ teaspoon lemon rind and ½ teaspoon lemon
juice in small bowl; spread over tapenade.
Top each panini with 4 slices coppa and
15g (½ ounce) rocket (arugula); drizzle with
1 teaspoon vinegar then top with roll halves.
Cook panini in preheated sandwich press until
browned lightly and heated through.

CROQUE-MONSIEUR

prep + cook time **25 minutes** serves **2**
nutritional count per sandwich **25.9g total fat**
(15g saturated fat); 2077kJ (497 cal);
38.4g carbohydrate; 24.8g protein; 5.8g fibre

Make cheese sauce. Spread sauce over
4 slices wholemeal bread; top two slices with
90g (3 ounces) ham then top with remaining
bread. Melt 20g (¾ ounce) butter in large frying
pan. Add sandwiches; cook, until browned
both sides. Cut into triangles to serve.
cheese sauce Melt 10g (½ ounce) butter in
small saucepan, add 2 teaspoons flour; cook,
stirring, until mixture bubbles and thickens.
Gradually add 5 tablespoons milk; cook,
stirring, until sauce boils and thickens.
Remove from heat; stir in ⅓ cup coarsely
grated cheddar cheese and 2 teaspoons finely
chopped fresh flat-leaf parsley.

SPINACH OMELETTE

prep + cook time **15 minutes** serves **2**
nutritional count per serving **5.7g total fat**
(1.6g saturated fat); 878kJ (210 cal);
21.2g carbohydrate; 16.3g protein; 4.0g fibre

Whisk 1 egg, 4 egg whites and 2 thinly sliced
green onions (scallions) in small jug.
Spray small frying pan with cooking oil; heat
pan. Pour egg mixture into pan; cook, tilting
pan, until mixture is almost set. Sprinkle
30g (1 ounce) baby spinach leaves and
2 tablespoons coarsely chopped fresh mint
over half the omelette; fold omelette over to
enclose filling, then cut in half. Spread 2 slices
toasted rye bread with 2 tablespoons low-fat
ricotta cheese; serve with omelette.

HERB & MUSHROOM OMELETTE

prep + cook time **30 minutes** serves **2**
nutritional count per serving **35.3g total fat**
(12.9g saturated fat); 1714kJ (410 cal);
1g carbohydrate; 22.4g protein; 1.8g fibre

Combine 1 tablespoon each finely chopped
fresh flat-leaf parsley, chervil, chives and tarragon
in small bowl. Heat 30g (1 ounce) butter in
medium frying pan. Add 250g (8 ounces) halved
swiss brown mushrooms; cook, stirring,
5 minutes. Remove from heat; stir in 1 teaspoon
finely grated lemon rind, 2 teaspoons lemon juice
and 1 tablespoon of herb mixture. Cover to keep
warm. Gently whisk 6 eggs and 2 tablespoons
water in a bowl, whisk in remaining herb mixture.
Heat 2 teaspoons of oil in medium frying pan.
Pour half the egg mixture into pan; cook over
medium heat, tilting pan, until egg is almost set.
Fold omelette in half. Cook 30 seconds then
slide onto plate. Repeat process with remaining
egg. Top with mushrooms.

EGGS

POTATO FRITTATA

prep + cook time **40 minutes** serves **2**
nutritional count per serving **34.1g total fat**
(15.2g saturated fat); 2031kJ (486 cal);
14.3g carbohydrate; 30.2g protein; 2.1g fibre

Preheat oven to 220°C/425°F.
Heat 1 tablespoon oil in small frying pan;
add 1 medium potato, cut into 1cm (½ inch)
pieces, cook, stirring occasionally, until browned
and tender. Add 1 thinly sliced green onion
(scallion); cook, stirring gently, 1 minute.
Meanwhile, whisk 4 eggs, 2 tablespoons
pouring cream, 2 tablespoons finely grated
parmesan cheese and 2 teaspoons finely
chopped dill in medium jug. Pour into pan; stir
gently. Cook frittata over medium heat, about
2 minutes or until bottom sets. Transfer to oven;
cook, uncovered, about 10 minutes or until
frittata sets. Slide frittata onto serving plate;
serve topped with 100g (3 ounces) smoked
salmon, 1 tablespoon sour cream and extra dill.

ASPARAGUS FRITTATA

prep + cook time **25 minutes** serves **2**
nutritional count per serving **6.3g total fat**
(1.8g saturated fat); 614kJ (147 cal);
5.4g carbohydrate; 16.3g protein; 1.9g fibre

Preheat grill (broiler). Spray small ovenproof
frying pan with cooking oil; cook 1 thinly sliced
small red onion over heat, stirring, 1 minute.
Cut 170g (5½ ounces) asparagus into 2.5cm
(1 inch) lengths. Add to pan; cook, stirring,
2 minutes. Meanwhile, combine 2 eggs, 2 egg
whites and 2 tablespoons low-fat cottage
cheese in a medium jug. Pour over asparagus
mixture in pan. Cook, uncovered, about
5 minutes or until frittata is browned underneath.
Place pan under grill for about 5 minutes or
until frittata is set. Combine 40g (1½ ounces)
baby rocket (arugula) leaves, 2 tablespoons
lemon juice and 2 teaspoons drained baby
capers in small bowl; serve frittata with salad.

HERBED CHICKEN SCHNITZEL

prep + cook time 30 minutes **serves** 2
nutritional count per serving 28.1g total fat
(5.9g saturated fat); 2746kJ (657 cal);
38.5g carbohydrate; 59.9g protein; 4.6g fibre

2 chicken breast fillets (400g)
2 tablespoons plain (all-purpose) flour
1 egg
1 tablespoon milk
1¼ cups (85g) stale white breadcrumbs
1 teaspoon finely grated lemon rind
1 tablespoon finely chopped fresh
    flat-leaf parsley
1 tablespoon finely chopped fresh basil
2 tablespoons finely grated
    parmesan cheese
vegetable oil, for shallow-frying
green bean salad
125g (4 ounces) baby green beans, trimmed
1 tablespoon lemon juice
2 teaspoons olive oil
2 tablespoons coarsely chopped fresh
    flat-leaf parsley

1 Using meat mallet, gently pound chicken,
one piece at a time, between sheets of
plastic wrap until 5mm (¼ inch) thick;
cut each piece in half.
2 Whisk flour, egg and milk in shallow bowl;
combine breadcrumbs, rind, herbs and
cheese in another shallow bowl.
Coat chicken pieces, one at a time,
in egg mixture then breadcrumb mixture.
3 Heat oil in medium frying pan; shallow-fry
chicken, until cooked. Drain on absorbent paper.
4 Meanwhile, make green bean salad; serve
salad with chicken, and lemon wedges.
green bean salad Boil, steam or microwave
beans until tender; drain. Toss beans in
medium bowl with remaining ingredients.

pork chops with apples and calvados

PORK CHOPS WITH APPLES AND CALVADOS

prep + cook time 30 minutes serves 2
nutritional count per serving 47.5g total fat
(25g saturated fat); 2947kJ (705 cal);
18.1g carbohydrate; 35.7g protein; 1.4g fibre

2 x 280g (9 ounce) pork loin chops
30g (1 ounce) butter
1 medium apple (150g), peeled,
    cut into thin wedges
2 shallots (50g), sliced thinly
2 teaspoons plain (all-purpose) flour
¼ cup (60ml) calvados
½ cup (125ml) cider vinegar
½ cup (125ml) chicken stock
⅓ cup (80ml) pouring cream

1 Cook pork in heated oiled medium frying pan.
Remove from pan; cover to keep warm.
Drain and discard excess fat from pan.
2 Heat half the butter in pan; cook apple,
stirring, until browned lightly. Remove from pan.
3 Heat remaining butter in pan; cook shallots,
stirring, until soft. Add flour; cook, stirring,
1 minute. Add calvados; bring to the boil.
Stir in cider, stock and cream; simmer,
uncovered, until sauce thickens slightly.
Return apples to pan; cook until heated through.
4 Serve pork topped with apple and sauce;
accompany with a green salad.

steak diane

STEAK DIANE

prep + cook time 20 minutes serves 2
nutritional count per serving 39.1g total fat
(21.6g saturated fat); 2182kJ (522 cal);
5.2g carbohydrate; 27.9g protein; 0.4g fibre

1 tablespoon olive oil
2 x 125g (4 ounce) beef fillet steaks
2 tablespoons brandy
1 clove garlic, crushed
1½ tablespoons worcestershire sauce
½ cup (125ml) pouring cream
2 teaspoons finely chopped fresh
    flat-leaf parsley

1 Heat oil in medium frying pan; cook steaks.
Remove from pan; cover to keep warm.
2 Add brandy to pan; bring to the boil.
Add garlic, sauce and cream; cook, stirring,
about 3 minutes or until sauce thickens slightly.
3 Remove from heat; stir in parsley. Serve
steaks with sauce, and accompany with
shoestring chips and a leafy green salad.

garlic prawns

1 Shell and devein prawns, leaving tails intact. Combine prawns, garlic and chilli in medium bowl.
2 Heat half the oil in large frying pan; cook prawns, stirring, until changed in colour. Remove from pan.
3 Heat remaining oil in same pan; cook capsicums, stirring, until tender. Return prawns to pan with stock, cream and juice; bring to the boil. Reduce heat; simmer, uncovered, about 5 minutes or until sauce thickens slightly. Remove from heat; stir in parsley.

GREEN CURRY WITH CHICKEN MEATBALLS

prep + cook time **50 minutes** serves 2
nutritional count per serving **80.5g total fat**
(44.7g saturated fat); 4243kJ (1015 cal);
19.7g carbohydrate; 50.6g protein; 9.1g fibre

400g (12½ ounces) minced (ground) chicken
1 clove garlic, crushed
1cm (½ inch) piece fresh ginger (5g), grated
1 tablespoon finely chopped fresh
    coriander (cilantro)
1 tablespoon peanut oil
1½ tablespoons green curry paste
1½ cups (375ml) coconut cream
1 tablespoon fish sauce
1 tablespoon lime juice
2 teaspoons grated palm sugar
90g (3 ounces) sugar snap peas, trimmed
½ cup (40g) bean sprouts
2 tablespoons fresh coriander (cilantro) leaves
⅓ cup (50g) roasted unsalted cashews
½ fresh long green chilli, sliced thinly

1 Combine chicken, garlic, ginger and chopped coriander in medium bowl; roll level tablespoons of mixture into balls.
2 Heat half the oil in medium frying pan; cook chicken balls until browned.
3 Meanwhile, heat remaining oil in medium saucepan; cook paste, stirring, about 1 minute or until fragrant. Add coconut cream, sauce, juice and sugar; bring to the boil. Reduce heat; simmer, uncovered, 15 minutes. Add balls to pan with peas; simmer, uncovered, until balls are cooked through and peas are tender.
4 Serve bowls of curry sprinkled with sprouts, coriander leaves, nuts and chilli.

GARLIC PRAWNS

prep + cook time **30 minutes** serves 2
nutritional count per serving **42.6g total fat**
(22.9g saturated fat); 2169kJ (519 cal);
5.4g carbohydrate; 28.9g protein; 1.4g fibre

500g (1 pound) uncooked medium king
    prawns (shrimp)
2 cloves garlic, crushed
1 fresh small red thai (serrano) chilli,
    chopped finely
1 tablespoon olive oil
1 small red capsicum (bell pepper) (150g),
    sliced thinly
1 small green capsicum (bell pepper) (150g),
    sliced thinly
¼ cup (60ml) chicken stock
⅔ cup (160ml) pouring cream
2 teaspoons lemon juice
2 teaspoons finely chopped fresh
    flat-leaf parsley

green curry with chicken meatballs

salt and sichuan pepper salmon with wasabi mayonnaise

SALT AND SICHUAN PEPPER SALMON WITH WASABI MAYONNAISE

prep + cook time **25 minutes** serves **2**
nutritional count per serving **40.1g total fat**
(6.3g saturated fat); 2278kJ (545 cal);
7.5g carbohydrate; 39.4 protein; 0.2g fibre

1 teaspoon sea salt
1 teaspoon sichuan pepper
1½ tablespoons vegetable oil
2 x 200g (6½ ounce) salmon fillets, skin on
¼ cup (75g) mayonnaise
1 teaspoon wasabi paste
1 teaspoon finely chopped fresh
**   coriander (cilantro)**
1 teaspoon lime juice

1 Using mortar and pestle or pepper grinder, grind salt and pepper until fine. Combine pepper mixture, half the oil and fish in medium bowl, cover; stand 5 minutes.
2 Meanwhile, combine mayonnaise, wasabi, coriander and juice in small bowl.
3 Heat remaining oil in medium frying pan; cook fish, skin-side down, until skin crisps. Turn fish; cook, uncovered, until cooked as desired.
4 Serve fish with wasabi mayonnaise and watercress.

pancetta and radicchio rigatoni

PANCETTA AND RADICCHIO RIGATONI

prep + cook time **25 minutes** serves **2**
nutritional count per serving **34.4g total fat**
(21.3g saturated fat); 3252kJ (778 cal);
96.9g carbohydrate; 22g protein; 8.2g fibre

250g (8 ounces) rigatoni pasta
3 slices pancetta (45g)
15g (½ ounce) butter
1 small leek (200g), sliced thinly
½ cup (125ml) pouring cream
1 medium radicchio (200g), sliced thinly
¼ cup fresh flat-leaf parsley leaves
1 teaspoon finely grated lemon rind
2 tablespoons lemon juice

1 Cook pasta in medium saucepan of boiling water, uncovered, until tender.
2 Meanwhile, cook pancetta in heated oiled medium frying pan until crisp; chop coarsely.
3 Melt butter in same frying pan; cook leek, stirring, until soft. Add cream; bring to a boil. Reduce heat; simmer, uncovered, 2 minutes.
4 Add leek mixture to drained pasta with half the pancetta and remaining ingredients; toss gently then sprinkle with remaining pancetta.

lamb cutlets nicoise

LAMB CUTLETS NICOISE

prep + cook time **30 minutes** serves 2
nutritional count per serving **33g total fat**
(8.8g saturated fat); 1852kJ (443 cal);
9.9g carbohydrate; 24.8g protein; 5.2g fibre

6 french-trimmed lamb cutlets (300g)
1 baby cos lettuce, chopped coarsely
½ x 400g (12½ ounce) can white beans,
  rinsed, drained
2 medium tomatoes (300g), cut into wedges
lemon anchovy dressing
2 anchovy fillets, drained, chopped finely
1 clove garlic, crushed
2 teaspoons finely grated lemon rind
2 tablespoons lemon juice
2 tablespoons olive oil

1 Make lemon anchovy dressing.
2 Combine lamb and 1 tablespoon of the
dressing in medium bowl.
3 Cook lamb in heated oiled medium frying
pan, uncovered, until cooked as desired.
Remove from heat; drizzle with 2 teaspoons
of the dressing, cover to keep warm.
4 Combine remaining dressing, lettuce,
beans and tomato in large bowl. Serve
lamb with salad.
lemon anchovy dressing Combine
ingredients in screw-top jar; shake well.

SALTIMBOCCA

prep + cook time **35 minutes** serves 2
nutritional count per serving **21.4g total fat**
(11.6g saturated fat); 1777kJ (425 cal);
0.3g carbohydrate; 47.5g protein; 0g fibre

4 x 100g (3 ounce) beef scotch fillet steaks
2 slices prosciutto (30g), halved crossways
4 fresh sage leaves
¼ cup (20g) finely grated pecorino cheese
30g (1 ounce) butter
½ cup (125ml) dry white wine
2 teaspoons coarsely chopped fresh sage

1 Place beef on board; using meat mallet,
flatten slightly. Centre one piece prosciutto,
one sage leaf and a quarter of the cheese
on each piece of beef; fold in half, secure with
a toothpick.
2 Melt half the butter in large frying pan;
cook saltimbocca about 5 minutes or until
cooked through. Remove from pan; cover
to keep warm.
3 Pour wine into same pan; bring to a boil.
Boil, uncovered, until liquid is reduced by half.
Stir in remaining butter and chopped sage.
4 Serve saltimbocca, drizzled with sauce, with
steamed baby green beans.
tip **You will need 4 toothpicks for this recipe**

saltimbocca

PRAWN AND CHORIZO SKEWERS WITH BEAN AND TOMATO SALAD

prep + cook time 35 minutes (+ refrigeration) serves 2
nutritional count per serving 49.9g total fat
(12.3g saturated fat); 2730kJ (653 cal);
5.4g carbohydrate; 45g protein; 3.4g fibre

12 uncooked medium king prawns
  (shrimp) (500g)
2 cloves garlic, crushed
1 tablespoon olive oil
90g (3 ounces) green beans, trimmed, halved
2 medium egg (plum) tomatoes (150g), sliced
1 tablespoon roasted pine nuts
1½ tablespoons coarsely chopped fresh
  flat-leaf parsley
4 x 20cm (8 inch) stalks fresh rosemary
1 chorizo sausage (170g), sliced thickly
lime mustard dressing
1 tablespoon olive oil
1 tablespoon lime juice
2 teaspoons wholegrain mustard
1 clove garlic, crushed

1 Shell and devein prawns, leaving tails intact.
Combine prawns in medium bowl with garlic
and oil. Cover; refrigerate 3 hours or overnight.
2 Make lime mustard dressing.
3 Meanwhile, boil, steam or microwave beans
until just tender; drain. Rinse under cold water;
drain. Combine beans in medium bowl with
tomato, nuts, parsley and dressing.
4 Drain prawns, discard marinade. Remove
leaves from bottom two-thirds of each
rosemary stalk; thread prawns and chorizo,
alternately, onto rosemary skewers. Cook
skewers in heated oiled grill pan until prawns
are changed in colour and chorizo is browned.
lime mustard dressing Combine ingredients
in screw-top jar; shake well.

GRILLS

za'atar spiced veal loin chops with fattoush

1 Preheat grill (broiler).
2 Make za'atar.
3 Make fattoush.
4 Grill veal until browned both sides and cooked. Sprinkle about a tablespoon of the za'atar equally over the veal; serve with fattoush.
za'atar Combine ingredients in small bowl.
fattoush Grill bread until crisp; break into small pieces. Combine tomato, cucumber, capsicum, onion and herbs in large bowl. Just before serving, toss bread and combined oil, juice and garlic into salad.

GRILLED LAMB WITH SPICY PEACH SALSA

prep + cook time **25 minutes** serves 2
nutritional count per serving 25.1g total fat
(8.6g saturated fat); 1881kJ (450 cal);
9.8g carbohydrate; 44.6g protein; 2.9g fibre

400g (12½ ounces) lamb backstraps
spicy peach salsa
½ small red onion (50g), chopped finely
1 large peach (220g), chopped finely
1 tablespoon finely chopped fresh
   flat-leaf parsley
½ fresh long red chilli, chopped finely
2 teaspoons malt vinegar
spinach salad
60g (2 ounces) baby spinach leaves
2 teaspoons malt vinegar
2 teaspoons olive oil
1 tablespoon roasted pine nuts
2 teaspoons dried currants

1 Cook lamb on heated oiled grill plate (or grill or barbecue) until cooked as desired. Stand, covered, 10 minutes then slice thinly.
2 Meanwhile, make spicy peach salsa and spinach salad.
3 Serve lamb with salsa and spinach salad.
spicy peach salsa Combine ingredients in small bowl; toss gently.
spinach salad Place spinach, vinegar, olive oil, nuts and currants in small bowl; toss to combine.

ZA'ATAR SPICED VEAL LOIN CHOPS WITH FATTOUSH

prep + cook time **35 minutes** serves 2
nutritional count per serving 38.9g total fat
(5.9g saturated fat); 2587kJ (619 cal);
27.8g carbohydrate; 36.5g protein; 17.1g fibre

2 x 200g (6½ ounce) veal loin chops
za'atar
2 teaspoons sumac
2 teaspoons roasted sesame seeds
1 teaspoon finely chopped fresh thyme
2 teaspoons olive oil
½ teaspoon dried marjoram
fattoush
1 large pitta bread (80g)
2 medium tomatoes (300g), cut into wedges
1 lebanese cucumber (130g), seeded,
   sliced thinly
1 small green capsicum (bell pepper) (150g),
   cut into 2.5cm (1 inch) pieces
1 green onion (scallion), sliced thinly
½ cup coarsely chopped fresh
   flat-leaf parsley
¼ cup coarsely chopped fresh mint
¼ cup (60ml) olive oil
1½ tablespoons lemon juice
1 clove garlic, crushed

grilled lamb with spicy peach salsa

teriyaki pork with pineapple

TERIYAKI PORK WITH PINEAPPLE

prep + cook time 35 minutes (+ refrigeration) serves 2
nutritional count per serving 12.2g total fat
(4.1g saturated fat); 1371kJ (328 cal);
13.3g carbohydrate; 34.1g protein; 3g fibre

2 tablespoons mirin
1½ tablespoons japanese soy sauce
1 tablespoon cooking sake
1 teaspoon white sugar
2.5cm (1 inch) piece fresh ginger (15g), grated
1 clove garlic, crushed
300g (9½ ounces) pork fillets
½ small pineapple (450g), sliced thinly
1 green onion (scallion), sliced thinly

1 Combine mirin, sauce, sake, sugar, ginger and garlic in medium bowl; add pork, turn to coat in marinade. Cover; refrigerate 3 hours or overnight.
2 Drain pork; reserve marinade. Cook pork on heated oiled grill plate (or grill or barbecue) until browned and cooked as desired. Cover; stand 10 minutes.
3 Cook pineapple on grill plate about 2 minutes or until soft.
4 Bring reserved marinade to a boil in small saucepan; cook about 2 minutes or until sauce reduces slightly.
5 Serve sliced pork with pineapple and onion; drizzle with sauce.

ROSEMARY AND PROSCIUTTO CHICKEN LEGS WITH CREAMY RISONI

prep + cook time 1 hour 15 minutes serves 2
nutritional count per serving 60.4g total fat
(29.2g saturated fat); 3783kJ (509 cal);
42.6g carbohydrate; 47.3g protein; 3.4g fibre

4 stalks fresh rosemary
4 chicken drumsticks (600g)
4 slices prosciutto (60g)
½ cup (110g) risoni
2 teaspoons olive oil
1 small brown onion (80g), chopped finely
1 small clove garlic, crushed
⅔ cup (160ml) pouring cream
pinch dried chilli flakes
125g (4 ounces) cherry tomatoes, halved
2 teaspoons fresh lemon thyme leaves

rosemary and prosciutto chicken legs with creamy risoni

1 Press one rosemary stalk onto each drumstick; firmly wrap one prosciutto slice around each to hold in place.
2 Cook chicken on heated oiled grill plate (or grill, or barbecue) until brown all over. Cover chicken; cook about 40 minutes or until cooked.
3 Meanwhile, cook risoni in medium saucepan of boiling water until just tender; drain. Rinse under cold water; drain.
4 Heat oil in medium frying pan; cook onion and garlic, stirring, until onion softens. Add cream and chilli; simmer, uncovered, until mixture thickens. Add risoni, tomato and half the thyme; cook, stirring, until tomato just softens. Serve with chicken; sprinkle with remaining thyme.

grilled mushrooms with tomato and basil salad

GRILLED MUSHROOMS WITH TOMATO AND BASIL SALAD

prep + cook time **20 minutes** serves **2**
nutritional count per serving **23.2g total fat**
(3.2g saturated fat); 1028kJ (246 cal);
3.4g carbohydrate; 4.6g protein; 4.3g fibre

2 flat mushrooms (160g)
**2 medium tomatoes (300g), seeded,
   chopped finely**
1 tablespoon olive oil
1 teaspoon balsamic vinegar
1 clove garlic, crushed
**½ cup loosely packed fresh basil leaves,
   shredded finely**
balsamic vinaigrette
1½ tablespoons olive oil
2 teaspoons balsamic vinegar

1 Combine mushrooms, tomato, oil, vinegar
and garlic in medium bowl.
2 Cook mushrooms and tomato on heated
oiled grill plate (or grill or barbecue).
3 Meanwhile, make balsamic vinaigrette.
4 Divide mushrooms among serving plates;
top with tomato and basil, drizzle with vinaigrette.
balsamic vinaigrette Combine ingredients in
screw-top jar; shake well.

BARRAMUNDI WITH TOMATO, CAPER AND WALNUT DRESSING

prep + cook time **30 minutes** serves **2**
nutritional count per serving **19.8g total fat**
(9.2g saturated fat); 1471kJ (352 cal);
2g carbohydrate; 40.1g protein; 1.9g fibre

2 x 185g (6 ounce) barramundi fillets
tomato, caper and walnut dressing
125g (4 ounces) cherry tomatoes
30g (1 ounce) butter
2 teaspoons finely grated lemon rind
1 teaspoon lemon juice
**1 teaspoon drained capers, rinsed,
   chopped finely**
1½ tablespoons finely chopped walnuts
¼ cup coarsely chopped fresh flat-leaf parsley

1 Make tomato, caper and walnut dressing.
2 Cook fish on heated oiled grill plate (or grill or
barbecue). Serve fish topped with dressing.
tomato, caper and walnut dressing Cook
tomato on heated oiled grill plate until tender.
Melt butter in small saucepan; add tomatoes
and remaining ingredients, stir until hot.

barramundi with tomato, caper and walnut dressing

BURGERS ITALIAN-STYLE

prep + cook time **40 minutes** serves 2
nutritional count per serving **34.9g total fat**
(9.3g saturated fat); 3357kJ (803 cal);
71.5g carbohydrate; 47.6g protein; 5.6g fibre

250g (8 ounces) minced (ground) chicken
2 tablespoons finely chopped drained
    sun-dried tomatoes
2 teaspoons finely chopped fresh basil
1 egg white
½ cup (35g) stale breadcrumbs
1 clove garlic, crushed
2 slices pancetta (30g)
2 small focaccia rolls (220g),
    halved horizontally
¼ cup (75g) mayonnaise
30g (1 ounce) baby rocket (arugula) leaves
60g (2 ounces) bocconcini, sliced thickly

1 Combine chicken in medium bowl with
tomato, basil, egg white, breadcrumbs and half
the garlic; shape mixture into two burgers.
2 Cook burgers on heated oiled grill plate
(or grill or barbecue) about 20 minutes or
until cooked.
3 Cook pancetta on grill plate until crisp. Drain.
4 Toast cut sides of focaccia on grill plate.
5 Combine mayonnaise with remaining garlic,
spread on focaccia bases; sandwich rocket,
burgers, pancetta and cheese between rolls.

PASTRAMI & CHEESE WRAP

prep + cook time **15 minutes** makes **6**
nutritional count per wrap **9.2g total fat**
(5.2g saturated fat); 782kJ (187 cal);
13.9g carbohydrate; 11.7g protein; 1.2g fibre

Place 2 mountain bread squares together,
spread with a rounded tablespoon of tomato
chutney. Top with 15g (½ ounce) baby spinach
leaves, ½ cup coarsely grated cheddar cheese
and 75g (2½ ounces) shaved pastrami or ham;
roll to enclose. Repeat with mountain bread
squares, tomato chutney, spinach, cheese and
pastrami to make another roll. Cut rolls into
thirds crossways to serve.

TURKEY & CRANBERRY WRAP

prep + cook time **5 minutes** serves **2**
nutritional count per serving **2.1g total fat**
(0.4g saturated fat); 849kJ (203 cal);
27.6g carbohydrate; 16.7g protein; 2.5g fibre

Spread 2 rye mountain bread wraps evenly
with 2 tablespoons cranberry sauce; top with
80g (2½ ounces) shaved turkey, 30g (1 ounce)
trimmed snow pea sprouts and 30g (1 ounce)
baby spinach leaves. Roll to enclose.
tip **Snow pea sprouts are often hard to get. Substitute**
with regular bean sprouts or any other kind you like.
By all means, use rocket (arugula), or any left-over
greens instead of the spinach.

WRAPS

RICOTTA, BASIL & HAM WRAP

prep + cook time **8 minutes** serves **2**
nutritional count per serving **4.7g total fat**
(2.3g saturated fat); 886kJ (212 cal);
24.1g carbohydrate; 16.1g protein; 3.7g fibre

Preheat sandwich press. Slice 2 small zucchini
lengthways into ribbons using a vegetable
peeler. Divide ¼ cup low-fat ricotta cheese
among wraps; top with zucchini, 75g
(2½ ounces) shaved ham and ¼ cup coarsely
chopped fresh basil. Roll to enclose. Toast
wraps in sandwich press for about 3 minutes;
cut in half to serve.

DIJON CHICKEN & SALAD WRAP

prep + cook time **25 minutes** serves **2**
nutritional count per serving **3.8g total fat**
(0.7g saturated fat); 932kJ (223 cal);
17.9g carbohydrate; 27.4g protein; 3.2g fibre

Spray 200g (6½ ounces) chicken breast fillets
with cooking oil; cook chicken in heated small
frying pan. Cool; shred coarsely. Combine
chicken in medium bowl with 1 tablespoon
skim-milk natural yogurt and 1 teaspoon dijon
mustard. Divide chicken mixture between 2 rye
mountain bread wraps; top with 30g (1 ounce)
baby spinach leaves, 1 thinly sliced small
tomato and 1 coarsely grated small carrot.
Roll to enclose filling.

49

All these recipes can be frozen for up to 3 months.
Cool to room temperature, transfer to an airtight container, label and date.
Thaw overnight in the refrigerator. Reheat in a saucepan until hot.

CREAMY PUMPKIN & POTATO SOUP

prep + cook time **35 minutes** serves **2 (+ freeze 2 serves)**
nutritional count per serving **29.3g total fat
(11.7g saturated fat); 2006kJ (480 cal);
41.4g carbohydrate; 10.7g protein; 5g fibre**

Heat 1 tablespoon olive oil in large saucepan;
cook 1 coarsely chopped medium brown onion
and 1 clove crushed garlic, stirring, until onion
softens. Add 600g (1¼ pounds) coarsely
chopped pumpkin, 2 medium coarsely
chopped potatoes, 2 cups water and 1½ cups
vegetable stock; bring to the boil. Reduce heat;
simmer, covered, about 20 minutes or until
vegetables are tender. Stand for 10 minutes.
Blend or process soup, in batches, until smooth.
Return soup to same pan; add ¼ cup pouring
cream and 2 teaspoons lemon juice. Reheat,
stirring, without boiling, until hot. Serve bowls
of soup topped with garlic and herb croutons.

BEEF & ONION CASSEROLE

prep + cook time **2 hours** serves **2 (+ freeze 2 serves)**
nutritional count per serving **21.2g total fat
(6.2g saturated fat); 2245kJ (537 cal);
17.4g carbohydrate; 56.8g protein; 4g fibre**

Coat 1kg (2 pounds) diced beef in ⅓ cup plain
(all-purpose) flour, shake away excess. Heat
1 tablespoon olive oil in large saucepan; cook
beef, in batches, until browned all over. Heat
1 tablespoon olive oil in same pan; cook
2 coarsely chopped small brown onions,
2 cloves crushed garlic and 150g (4½ ounces)
quartered button mushrooms, stirring, until
onion softens. Return beef to pan with 1 cup
dry red wine, 400g (12½ ounces) canned
undrained crushed tomatoes, 2 cups beef
stock and 2 tablespoons tomato paste; bring
to a boil. Reduce heat; simmer, covered,
40 minutes. Uncover; simmer about 40 minutes
or until meat is tender and sauce thickens
slightly, stirring occasionally.

COOK & FREEZE

MEXICAN CHICKEN

prep + cook time **45 minutes** serves **2 (+ freeze 2 serves)**
nutritional count per serving **28.3g total fat**
(7g saturated fat); 2345kJ (561 cal);
19g carbohydrate; 54.1g protein; 8.1g fibre

Cook 1kg (2 pounds) coarsely chopped
chicken thigh fillets, in batches, in heated
oiled large deep frying pan, until browned.
Remove from pan. Heat 1 tablespoon olive oil
in same pan; cook 1 finely chopped medium
brown onion and 3 crushed garlic cloves,
stirring, until onion softens. Return chicken
to pan with 800g (1½ pounds) canned chopped
tomatoes and 1 cup chicken stock; bring to
the boil. Reduce heat; simmer, covered, about
25 minutes or until sauce thickens slightly.
Add ¼ cup drained sliced jalapeño chillies
and 420g (13½ ounces) canned kidney beans,
rinsed and drained; stir until mixture is
heated through. Serve sprinkled with fresh
oregano leaves.

MAPLE-GLAZED LAMB SHANKS

prep + cook time **2¼ hours** serves **2 (+ freeze 2 serves)**
nutritional count per serving **15.7g total fat**
(7.1g saturated fat); 2002kJ (479 cal);
25.7g carbohydrate; 58.9g protein; 0.3g fibre

Combine ⅓ cup pure maple syrup, 1 cup
chicken stock, 1 tablespoon dijon mustard and
1½ cups orange juice in large deep flameproof
casserole dish. Add 8 french-trimmed lamb
shanks; toss lamb to coat in syrup mixture.
Bring to the boil then cover tightly. Reduce heat;
cook lamb, turning every 20 minutes, about
2 hours or until lamb is tender. Serve with
roasted potatoes and wilted baby spinach leaves.

ROASTED LEMON
AND HERB CHICKEN

prep + cook time 1 hour 10 minutes **serves** 2
nutritional count per serving 26.5g total fat
(7.1g saturated fat); 1944kJ (465 cal);
21.2g carbohydrate; 28.9g protein; 4.5g fibre

500g (1 pound) small chicken
350g (11 ounces) pontiac potatoes,
   cut into 2.5cm (1 inch)-thick slices
1 tablespoon olive oil
1 lemon, cut into wedges
2 tablespoons fresh thyme sprigs
2 tablespoons fresh oregano leaves
¼ cup (60ml) dry white wine
1 tablespoon rinsed, drained baby capers

1 Preheat oven to 220°C/425°F.
2 Rinse chicken under cold water; pat dry with
absorbent paper. Using kitchen scissors, cut
along both sides of backbone; discard. Cut
chicken in half; place chicken, skin-side up,
and potato, in single layer, in medium shallow
baking dish. Drizzle with oil and juice from half
the lemon. Add remaining lemon wedges to
dish; sprinkle with herbs.
3 Roast, uncovered, 50 minutes. Add wine
and capers to dish; roast, uncovered, about
10 minutes or until chicken is cooked. Sprinkle
with extra fresh oregano leaves.

MINI
ROASTS
AND
BAKES

veal and asparagus with basil mayo

VEAL AND ASPARAGUS WITH BASIL MAYO

prep + cook time **30 minutes** serves **2**
nutritional count per serving **20.8g total fat**
(3.3g saturated fat); 1522kJ (364 cal);
8.5g carbohydrate; 35.3g protein; 1.2g fibre

2 x 170g (5½ ounce) veal cutlets
8 fresh basil leaves
2 slices prosciutto (30g)
170g (5½ ounces) asparagus, trimmed
2 teaspoons olive oil
basil mayonnaise
¼ cup (75g) mayonnaise
2 tablespoons finely chopped fresh
  basil leaves
2 teaspoons lemon juice

1 Preheat oven to 200°C/400°F.
2 Oil two oven trays. Place cutlets on one tray;
top with basil and prosciutto. Roast, uncovered,
20 minutes or until cutlets are cooked as desired.
3 Place asparagus on remaining tray, drizzle
with oil; roast, uncovered, for last 10 minutes of
cutlet cooking time.
4 Meanwhile, make basil mayonnaise.
5 Serve veal and asparagus drizzled with
basil mayonnaise.
basil mayonnaise Combine ingredients in
small bowl until smooth.

LIME AND CHILLI ROASTED SNAPPER

prep + cook time **30 minutes** serves **2**
nutritional count per serving **15.1g total fat**
(3.5g saturated fat); 1354kJ (324 cal);
55g carbohydrate; 40.6g protein; 1.8g fibre

2 x 500g (1 pound) plate-sized snapper, cleaned
1cm (½ inch) piece fresh ginger (5g),
  sliced thinly
1 clove garlic, sliced thinly
4 fresh kaffir lime leaves
½ fresh long red chilli, sliced thinly
1 tablespoon peanut oil
½ cup loosely packed fresh coriander
  (cilantro) leaves
lime and chilli dressing
2 tablespoons sweet chilli sauce
1½ tablespoons fish sauce
1½ tablespoons lime juice
1 teaspoon peanut oil

1 Preheat oven to 240°C/475°F.
2 Rinse fish inside and out under cold water;
pat dry with absorbent paper.
3 Divide ginger, garlic, lime leaves and chilli
among fish cavities; rub fish all over with oil.
4 Place fish in shallow oiled baking dish;
roast, uncovered, about 15 minutes or until
cooked through.
5 Meanwhile, make lime and chilli dressing.
6 Drizzle fish with dressing, sprinkle with
coriander leaves.
7 Serve with steamed asian greens.
lime and chilli dressing Combine ingredients
in screw-top jar; shake well.

lime and chilli roasted snapper

lamb racks with maple mustard glaze

LAMB RACKS WITH MAPLE MUSTARD GLAZE

prep + cook time **30 minutes** serves **2**
nutritional count per serving 26.2g **total fat**
(13.8g saturated fat); 2153kJ (515 cal);
44.4g carbohydrate; 22.8g protein; 5.5g fibre

2 x 4 french-trimmed lamb cutlet racks (360g)
1 clove garlic, sliced thinly
1 medium parsnip (250g),
   cut into 2.5cm (1 inch) cubes
1 small kumara (orange sweet potato) (250g),
   cut into 2.5cm (1 inch) cubes
¼ cup loosely packed fresh flat-leaf
   parsley leaves
maple mustard glaze
30g (1 ounce) butter
2 tablespoons maple syrup
1 tablespoon wholegrain mustard

1 Preheat oven to 200°C/400°F.
2 Make maple mustard glaze.
3 Meanwhile, using sharp knife, make cuts in lamb; press garlic slices into cuts. Place lamb in medium oiled baking dish; brush with 1 tablespoon of the glaze.
4 Combine remaining glaze, parsnip and kumara in medium bowl.
5 Place vegetables in baking dish with lamb; roast, uncovered, about 15 minutes or until vegetables are tender and lamb is cooked as desired. Stir parsley into vegetables; serve with lamb.
maple mustard glaze Combine ingredients in small saucepan; cook, stirring, until slightly thickened.

chicken margherita

CHICKEN MARGHERITA

prep + cook time **30 minutes** serves **2**
nutritional count per serving 28.7g **total fat**
(10.5g saturated fat); 2144kJ (513 cal);
3g carbohydrate; 59.7g protein; 2.3g fibre

250g (8 ounces) baby vine-ripened
   truss tomatoes
2 x 200g (6½ ounces) chicken breast fillets
2 tablespoons basil pesto
90g (3 ounces) bocconcini cheese, sliced thinly
15g (½ ounce) baby spinach leaves
4 slices prosciutto (60g)

1 Preheat oven to 220°C/425°F.
2 Remove two tomatoes from truss; slice thinly.
3 Split one chicken fillet in half horizontally; open out. Spread half the pesto on one side of chicken fillet; top with half the cheese, sliced tomato and spinach. Fold chicken fillet over filling; wrap with two slices prosciutto to enclose securely. Repeat process with remaining chicken, pesto, cheese, sliced tomato, spinach and prosciutto.
4 Roast chicken and remaining tomatoes in medium oiled shallow baking dish, uncovered, about 20 minutes or until cooked through. Serve chicken with roasted tomatoes.

coconut fish with chips and lemon coriander mayo

COCONUT FISH WITH CHIPS AND LEMON CORIANDER MAYO

prep + cook time **1 hour** serves **2**
nutritional count per serving 12.9g total fat
(5.1g saturated); 2186kJ (523 cal);
55.6g carbohydrate; 41.6g protein; 7.2g fibre

500g (1 pound) coliban potatoes
cooking-oil spray
2 tablespoons desiccated coconut
⅓ cup (25g) stale breadcrumbs, toasted
1 teaspoon finely grated lemon rind
1 egg white
1 tablespoon low-fat milk
2 perch fillets (360g)
2 tablespoons plain (all-purpose) flour
lemon coriander mayo
¼ cup (75g) low-fat mayonnaise
2 teaspoons finely chopped fresh
    coriander (cilantro)
1 teaspoon finely grated lemon rind
2 teaspoons lemon juice

1 Preheat oven to 220°C/400°F.
2 Cut potatoes into 1cm (½ inch)-thick slices;
cut slices into 1cm (½ inch)-thick chips.
Place chips, in single layer, on baking paper
(parchment) lined oven tray; spray with cooking
oil. Roast about 40 minutes or until browned
and crisp.
3 Meanwhile, combine coconut, breadcrumbs
and rind in shallow small bowl. Whisk egg
white and milk in another shallow small bowl.
Coat fish in flour; shake off excess. Dip fish in
egg white mixture then coat in breadcrumb
mixture. Place on prepared tray; spray with
cooking-oil. Cook for final 20 minutes of chips'
cooking time.
4 Make lemon coriander mayonnaise. Serve
mayonnaise with fish and chips.
lemon coriander mayo Combine ingredients
in small bowl until smooth.
tip We've used perch, but you can use any firm white
fish you like.

tomato mustard beef with baby fennel

TOMATO MUSTARD BEEF WITH BABY FENNEL

prep + cook time **35 minutes** serves **2**
nutritional count per serving 24.7g total fat
(11.3g saturated fat); 2378kJ (569 cal);
23.2g carbohydrate; 59.9g protein; 6.7g fibre

¼ cup (60ml) chicken stock
1 clove garlic, crushed
500g (1 pound) piece beef eye fillet,
    halved horizontally
2 baby fennel (260g), trimmed, halved
2 tablespoons wholegrain mustard
¼ cup (30g) semi-dried tomatoes, drained,
    chopped finely
½ cup (35g) stale breadcrumbs
15g (½ ounce) butter, melted

1 Preheat oven to 240°C/475°F.
2 Place stock and garlic in small baking dish;
add beef and fennel.
3 Combine mustard, tomato, breadcrumbs
and melted butter in small bowl; press over
beef. Cook beef, uncovered, about 20 minutes
or until cooked as desired. Serve beef, drizzled
with pan juices and fennel.

mini baked ricotta with roast vegetables

MINI BAKED RICOTTA WITH ROAST VEGETABLES

prep + cook time **30 minutes** serves **2**
nutritional count per serving **21.7g total fat**
(10.5g saturated fat); 1438kJ (344 cal);
12.3g carbohydrate; 22.7g protein; 5.2g fibre

250g (8 ounces) ricotta cheese
¼ cup (20g) finely grated parmesan cheese
1 egg
2 tablespoons finely chopped fresh oregano
1 teaspoon finely grated lemon rind
½ fresh long red thai chilli, chopped finely
2 baby eggplants (120g), quartered
200g (6½ ounces) baby carrots, trimmed
1 small red capsicum (bell pepper) (150g),
  sliced thickly
1 tablespoon lemon juice
1 teaspoon olive oil
1 teaspoon fresh oregano leaves

1 Preheat oven to 220°C/425°F. Oil two holes of 6-hole (¾-cup/180ml) texas muffin pan.
2 Combine cheeses, egg, oregano, rind and chilli in medium bowl; divide mixture among pan holes. Bake, uncovered, about 20 minutes or until browned lightly and firm.
3 Meanwhile, combine eggplant, carrots, capsicum, juice and oil in medium oiled shallow baking dish; roast, uncovered, 20 minutes or until tender. Sprinkle ricotta with oregano leaves; serve with vegetables.

FREE-FORM CARAMELISED LEEK TART

prep + cook time **1 hour 20 minutes** serves **2**
nutritional count per serving **70g total fat**
(34.3g saturated fat); 4531kJ (1084 cal);
83.2g carbohydrate; 28.3g protein; 7.1g fibre

1 tablespoon olive oil
1 medium brown onion (150g), sliced thinly
1 medium leek (350g), trimmed, sliced thinly
2 teaspoons fresh thyme leaves
1 cup (240g) ricotta cheese
2 tablespoons coarsely grated
  parmesan cheese
1 egg, separated
2 sheets ready-rolled shortcrust pastry

1 Heat oil in medium frying pan; cook onion and leek, stirring, about 15 minutes or until mixture starts to caramelise. Stir in thyme; cool.
2 Meanwhile, combine ricotta, parmesan and egg yolk in small bowl.
3 Preheat oven to 200°C/400°F. Oil an oven tray; line with baking paper (parchment).
4 Using 20cm (8 inch) plate as a guide, cut 1 round from each pastry sheet; place rounds on tray. Divide ricotta mixture among rounds, leaving 4cm (1½ inch) border around edges.
5 Divide leek mixture over rounds. Turn border of each tart up around filling; brush upturned edges with egg white. Bake about 35 minutes or until pastry is browned lightly.

free-form caramelised leek tart

BANANA SPLIT

prep + cook time 30 minutes serves 2
nutritional count per serving 60.1g total fat
(31.7g saturated fat); 3618kJ (865 cal);
65.7g carbohydrate; 9.9g protein; 5.8g fibre

2 medium bananas (400g),
   halved lengthways
1 tablespoon light brown sugar
60g (2 ounces) dark eating chocolate
   (semi-sweet)
⅔ cup (160ml) thickened (heavy) cream
2 teaspoons dark rum
2 scoops (120ml) vanilla ice-cream
2 scoops (120ml) chocolate ice-cream
⅓ cup (40g) coarsely chopped
   roasted pecans
2 tablespoons toasted shredded coconut

1 Preheat grill (broiler).
2 Place bananas, cut-sides up, on oven tray;
sprinkle with sugar. Grill about 3 minutes or
until sugar melts.
3 Meanwhile, melt chocolate with 1 tablespoon
of the cream in small bowl set over small
saucepan of simmering water.
4 Beat remaining cream with rum in small bowl
with electric mixer until soft peaks form.
5 Place 2 banana halves in each of the two
dishes; top each with a scoop of the vanilla
and chocolate ice-cream. Top each with cream;
drizzle with chocolate then sprinkle with nuts
and coconut.

DESSERTS

date and apricot creamy rice

BERRY HAZELNUT CRUMBLES

prep + cook time **30 minutes** serves **2**
nutritional count per serving **14.6g total fat**
(3.2g saturated fat); 915kJ (219 cal);
16.8g carbohydrate; 4.8g protein; 3.9g fibre

1 cup (150g) frozen mixed berries
2 teaspoons lemon juice
1 tablespoon light brown sugar
¼ cup (30g) finely chopped roasted hazelnuts
1 tablespoon plain (all-purpose) flour
15g (½ ounce) cold butter, softened
2 tablespoons rolled oats

1 Preheat oven to 220°C/425°F. Grease two shallow ¾-cup (180ml) ovenproof dishes; place on oven tray.
2 Combine berries, juice, half the sugar and half the nuts in small bowl; divide mixture among dishes.
3 Combine remaining sugar and nuts with flour and butter until ingredients come together; stir in oats. Sprinkle over berry mixture.
4 Bake, uncovered, about 20 minutes or until browned lightly.

DATE AND APRICOT CREAMY RICE

prep + cook time **55 minutes** serves **2**
nutritional count per serving **9.6g total fat**
(4.6g saturated fat); 1480kJ (354 cal);
56.5g carbohydrate; 8.6g protein; 2.4g fibre

2 cups (500ml) milk
⅓ cup (75g) caster (superfine) sugar
½ cinnamon stick
1 teaspoon finely grated lemon rind
¼ cup (50g) uncooked arborio rice
¼ cup (30g) coarsely chopped dried apricots
¼ cup (60g) coarsely chopped fresh dates
1½ tablespoons coarsely chopped roasted
   unsalted pistachios

1 Combine milk, sugar, cinnamon and rind in small saucepan; bring to the boil. Gradually stir rice into boiling milk mixture. Reduce heat; simmer, covered, stirring occasionally, about 45 minutes or until rice is tender and liquid is almost absorbed.
2 Discard cinnamon stick; stir in apricots and dates, sprinkle with nuts.

berry hazelnut crumbles

individual tiramisu

INDIVIDUAL TIRAMISU

prep + cook time **20 minutes (+ refrigeration)** serves **2**
nutritional count per serving **49.5g total fat**
31.8g saturated fat); 2805kJ (671 cal);
48.3g carbohydrate; 9g protein; 0.4g fibre

1 teaspoon white sugar
1½ teaspoons instant coffee granules
1 teaspoon cocoa powder, sifted
½ cup (125ml) boiling water
125g (4 ounces) cream cheese, softened
⅔ cup (160ml) pouring cream
⅓ cup (55g) icing (confectioners') sugar
3 sponge-finger biscuits (45g)
1 teaspoon cocoa powder, extra

1 Blend white sugar, coffee and cocoa with the water in small bowl; cool.
2 Beat cheese in small bowl with electric mixer until smooth. Add cream and icing sugar; beat until smooth.
3 Halve biscuits crossways; dip in coffee mixture. Divide half the biscuits among two 1¼-cup (310ml) glasses. Divide half the cream mixture among glasses; top with remaining biscuits then remaining cream mixture. Refrigerate 30 minutes. Serve dusted with sifted extra cocoa powder.

caramel fondue with fresh fruit

CARAMEL FONDUE WITH FRESH FRUIT

prep + cook time **10 minutes** serves **2**
nutritional count per serving **27.7g total fat**
(18.2g saturated fat); 2002kJ (479 cal);
52.8g carbohydrate; 3.3g protein; 4.6g fibre

¼ cup (55g) firmly packed light brown sugar
⅓ cup (80ml) pouring cream
30g (1 ounce) butter
125g (4 ounces) strawberries, halved
1 medium banana (200g), sliced thickly
1 small pear (180g), sliced thinly

1 Combine sugar, cream and butter in small saucepan. Cook, stirring, until sugar dissolves and butter melts; bring to the boil.
2 Remove from heat; cool 5 minutes before serving with fruit.

choc-peanut bombes

WALNUT AND RICOTTA STUFFED FIGS

prep + cook time **15 minutes** serves **2**
nutritional count per serving **22.8g total fat**
(12.2g saturated fat); 1526kJ (365 cal);
32.6g carbohydrate; 6g protein; 3.1g fibre

4 medium figs (240g)
1½ tablespoons roasted walnuts,
    chopped coarsely
¼ cup (60g) ricotta cheese
2 teaspoons caster (superfine) sugar
2 tablespoons pouring cream
15g (½ ounce) butter
2 tablespoons light brown sugar

1 Preheat oven to 200°C/400°F.
2 Cut figs, from the top, into quarters, being careful not to cut all the way through; open slightly. Place on oven tray.
3 Combine nuts, cheese and sugar in small bowl; divide nut mixture among figs. Cook, uncovered, about 10 minutes or until figs are heated through.
4 Meanwhile, combine remaining ingredients in small saucepan; stir over heat until sugar dissolves.
5 Place two figs in each serving dish; drizzle with caramel sauce.

CHOC-PEANUT BOMBES

prep + cook time **5 minutes (+ refrigeration)** serves **2**
nutritional count per serving **46.8g total fat**
(27.5g saturated fat); 2475kJ (592 cal);
35g carbohydrate; 7.5g protein; 3.1g fibre

⅔ cup (160ml) thickened (heavy) cream
60g (2 ounces) dark eating (semi sweet)
    chocolate, melted
1½ tablespoons coarsely chopped
    unsalted peanuts
60g (2 ounce) snickers bar, chopped finely

1 Beat cream in small bowl with electric mixer until soft peaks form; add cooled chocolate, beat until combined. Fold in remaining ingredients; transfer mixture to loaf pan. Cover pan with foil; refrigerate 2 hours.

walnut and ricotta stuffed figs

BLACKBERRY SOUFFLES

prep + cook time **30 minutes (+ refrigeration)** serves **2**
nutritional count per serving **0.2g total fat**
(0g saturated fat); 510kJ (122 cal);
25.3g carbohydrate; 3.3g protein; 4.6g fibre

1 cup (150g) frozen blackberries
1 tablespoon water
2 tablespoons caster (superfine) sugar
2 egg whites
2 teaspoons icing (confectioners') sugar

1 Preheat oven to 200°C/400°F.
2 Combine blackberries and the water in small saucepan; bring to a boil. Reduce heat; simmer, uncovered, until blackberries soften. Add caster sugar, stir over medium heat, without boiling, until sugar dissolves; bring to a boil. Reduce heat; simmer, uncovered, 3 minutes. Remove from heat; using the back of a large spoon, push blackberry mixture through sieve into small bowl, discarding seeds in sieve. Refrigerate 15 minutes.
3 Beat egg whites in small bowl with electric mixer until soft peaks form. Fold in blackberry mixture until combined.
4 Divide mixture among two lightly greased 1-cup (250ml) ovenproof dishes; place on oven tray. Bake, uncovered about 12 minutes or until soufflés are puffed and browned lightly. Dust with sifted icing sugar; serve immediately.

BAKED BEANS, BACON, TOMATO & CHIVES ON TOASTED TURKISH

prep + cook time **15 minutes** serves **2**
nutritional count per serving **10.4g total fat**
(3.2g saturated fat); 1450kJ (347 cal);
34.5g carbohydrate; 22g protein; 7.4g fibre

Preheat grill (broiler). Combine 1 coarsely chopped medium tomato and 2 teaspoons finely chopped fresh chives in small bowl. Heat ½ x 420g (13½ ounce) can baked beans in tomato sauce in small saucepan. Meanwhile, cook 2 coarsely chopped rindless bacon slices, stirring, in heated small frying pan until crisp; drain on absorbent paper. Toast cut sides of roll. Top toast with beans, bacon and tomato mixture; grill about 2 minutes or until hot.

LEMON CHICKEN ON CIABATTA

prep + cook time **15 minutes** serves **2**
nutritional count per serving **20.1g total fat**
(3.8g saturated fat); 1438kJ (344 cal);
15.8g carbohydrate; 24.5g protein; 1.3g fibre

Bring 2 cups water to the boil in medium frying pan; add 200g (6½ ounces) chicken breast fillets. Reduce heat; simmer, covered, about 10 minutes or until chicken is cooked. Cool chicken in poaching liquid 10 minutes; drain, shred chicken finely. Meanwhile, preheat grill (broiler). Brush 4 thick slices ciabatta bread on both sides with combined 1 tablespoon olive oil and 1 small clove crushed garlic; toast, both sides, under grill. Meanwhile, combine 1 tablespoon olive oil, 1 teaspoon finely grated lemon rind, ½ finely chopped fresh long red chilli and 1 tablespoon finely chopped fresh flat-leaf parsley in a medium bowl. Add chicken and toss to combine; divide among toasts.

CHEESY SCRAMBLED EGGS WITH SPINACH

prep + cook time **10 minutes** serves **2**
nutritional count per serving **13.8g total fat**
(5.4g saturated fat); 790kJ (189 cal); 1g carbohydrate;
15.3g protein; 0.3g fibre

Whisk 4 eggs in medium bowl until combined then whisk in 2 tablespoons reduced-fat spreadable cream cheese and 30g (1 ounce) coarsely chopped baby spinach leaves. Cook mixture, stirring gently, in heated oiled small frying pan over low heat until almost set. Serve with wholemeal toast.

TANDOORI LAMB PIZZA

prep + cook time **35 minutes** serves **2**
nutritional count per serving **25.2g total fat**
(8.7g saturated fat); 3954kJ (946 cal);
112.7g carbohydrate; 50.3g protein; 10.9g fibre

Preheat oven to 220°C/425°F. Combine 1½ tablespoons yogurt, 1½ tablespoons tandoori paste and 300g (9½ ounces) lamb backstraps in small bowl. Heat 15g (½ ounce) butter in medium saucepan; cook 1 thickly sliced medium red onion and 1 clove crushed garlic, stirring, about 10 minutes or until onion is caramelised. Place a 335g (10½ ounce) 25cm (10 inch) pizza base on oven tray; spread with ¼ cup mango chutney then top with onion and 2 tablespoons coarsely chopped raisins. Cook about 15 minutes or until base is crisp. Meanwhile, cook lamb on heated oiled grill plate (or grill or barbecue) until cooked as desired. Cover; stand 5 minutes then slice thinly. Top pizza with lamb, 1 tablespoon yogurt and 2 tablespoons fresh coriander (cilantro) leaves.

SUNDAY NIGHT SUPPERS

LENTIL SOUP

prep + cook time **40 minutes** serves **2**
nutritional count per serving **13.4g total fat**
(3.7g saturated fat); 1484kJ (355 cal);
27.8g carbohydrate; 26.1g protein; 10.1g fibre

Heat 2 teaspoons oil in medium saucepan;
cook 2 coarsely chopped rindless bacon slices,
1 finely chopped small brown onion, 1 finely
chopped small carrot and ½ finely chopped
celery stalk, stirring, until onion softens.
Add ½ cup brown lentils, ½ x 400g (12½ ounce)
can undrained crushed tomatoes, 2 cups
chicken stock and 1 bay leaf; bring to the boil.
Reduce heat; simmer, covered, 20 minutes or
until lentils are tender. Discard bay leaf; serve
soup sprinkled with 1 tablespoon finely
chopped fresh flat-leaf parsley.

POACHED EGGS WITH
ASPARAGUS & WALNUT SALAD

prep + cook time **20 minutes** serves **2**
nutritional count per serving **38.5g total fat**
(8g saturated fat); 2282kJ (546 cal);
23.4g carbohydrate; 25.1g protein; 4.8g fibre

Combine 1½ tablespoons olive oil, 1 teaspoon
finely grated lime rind, 2 teaspoons lime juice
and 1 teaspoon finely chopped fresh dill in
screw-top jar; shake well. Trim and halve
250g (8 ounces) asparagus. Boil, steam or
microwave asparagus until tender; drain.
Combine asparagus, ¼ cup coarsely chopped
roasted walnuts, ¼ cup coarsely grated
parmesan cheese and 125g halved yellow
teardrop tomatoes with dressing in a medium
bowl. Divide asparagus mixture among serving
plates. Poach 4 eggs until barely set.
Toast ½ thinly sliced small french bread stick.
Top salad with eggs, serve with toast.

STEAK SANDWICH REVISITED

prep + cook time **15 minutes** serves **2**
nutritional count per serving **15g total fat**
(6.6g saturated fat); 1768kJ (423 cal);
35.5g carbohydrate; 34.7g protein; 2.9g fibre

Cook 2 125g (4 ounce) eye fillet steaks,
uncovered, in heated oiled small frying pan until
cooked as desired. Cover; stand 5 minutes
then slice thinly. Meanwhile, slice 1 small french
bread stick lengthways, do not cut all the way
through; halve crossways. Fill each of the 2 bread
pieces with equal amounts of 30g (1 ounce)
trimmed watercress, sliced beef and combined
1 tablespoon horseradish cream and
1 tablespoon sour cream.

CHICKEN, BOCCONCINI
& OLIVE PIZZA

prep + cook time **35 minutes** serves **2**
nutritional count per serving **24.2g total fat**
(8.7g saturated fat); 3407kJ (815 cal);
96.7g carbohydrate; 47.4g protein; 8.3g fibre

Preheat oven to 240°C/475°F. Cook 200g
(6½ ounces) chicken breast fillets, uncovered,
in heated oiled small frying pan until cooked
through. Remove from pan; slice thinly.
Meanwhile, place a 335g (10½ ounce) 25cm
(10 inch) pizza base on oven tray; spread
¼ cup bottled tomato pasta sauce over base.
Sprinkle chicken, ¼ cup seeded black olives,
125g (4 ounces) halved cherry tomatoes and
100g (3 ounces) thinly sliced cherry bocconcini
over bases. Bake about 15 minutes or until
base is crisp. Drizzle 1 tablespoon pesto over
pizza, sprinkle with ¼ cup firmly packed fresh
basil leaves.

BEAN SPROUTS also known as bean shoots; tender new growths of beans and seeds germinated for consumption as sprouts. Most readily available are mung bean, soy bean, alfalfa and snow pea sprouts.

BEANS

borlotti also known as roman beans or pink beans; can be eaten fresh or dried. Interchangeable with pinto beans because of the similarity in appearance – both are pale pink or beige with dark red streaks.

white in this book, some recipes may simply call for "white beans", a generic term we use for canned or dried cannellini, haricot, navy or great northern beans.

BEEF EYE FILLET tenderloin fillet with a fine texture; is extremely tender and expensive.

BREADCRUMBS

fresh usually white bread that is processed into crumbs.

packaged prepared fine-textured but crunchy white breadcrumbs.

stale crumbs made by blending or processing 1- or 2-day-old bread.

BROCCOLINI a cross between broccoli and chinese kale; long asparagus-like stems with a long loose floret, both completely edible. Resembles broccoli in look but is milder and sweeter in taste.

BUTTERMILK sold in the dairy section in supermarkets. Originally the term given to the slightly sour liquid left after butter was churned from cream, today it is commercially made similarly to yogurt.

CALVADOS apple-flavoured brandy.

CAPSICUM also known as bell pepper or pepper. Seeds and membranes should be discarded before use.

CHEESE

blue mould-treated cheeses mottled with blue veining. Varieties include firm and crumbly stilton types and mild, creamy brie-like cheeses.

bocconcini the term used for walnut-sized baby mozzarella; a delicate, semi-soft, white cheese. *Cherry bocconcini* are smaller than regular mozzarella. Both spoil rapidly so must be kept, under refrigeration, in brine, for no more than 2 days.

fetta a crumbly goat- or sheep-milk cheese with a sharp salty taste.

haloumi a firm, cream-coloured sheep-milk cheese matured in brine. Somewhat like a minty, salty fetta in flavour; can be grilled or fried, briefly, without breaking down.

mozzarella soft, spun-curd cheese generally made from cow milk; has a low melting point and elastic properties when heated. Is used for texture rather than flavour.

pizza commercial blend of varying proportions of processed grated mozzarella, cheddar and parmesan.

ricotta a soft, sweet, moist, white cow-milk cheese with a low fat content and a slightly grainy texture. The name roughly translates as "cooked again" and refers to ricotta's manufacture from a whey that is itself a by-product of other cheese making.

CHINESE COOKING WINE also called shao hsing or chinese rice wine; made from fermented rice, wheat, sugar and salt with a 13.5 per cent alcohol content. Found in Asian food shops; if you can't find it, replace with mirin or sherry.

CHORIZO SAUSAGE of Spanish origin; made of coarsely ground pork and highly seasoned with garlic and chilli.

CHOY SUM also known as pakaukeo or flowering cabbage, a member of the buk choy family; easy to identify with its long stems, light green leaves and yellow flowers. Stems and leaves are both edible, steamed or stir-fried.

COCONUT

cream obtained commercially from the first pressing of the coconut flesh alone, without the addition of water. Available in cans and cartons at most supermarkets.

flaked dried flaked coconut flesh.

flavoured-liqueur we use Malibu.

milk not the liquid found inside the fruit (known as coconut water), but the diluted liquid (less rich) from the second pressing of the white flesh of a mature coconut. Available in cans and cartons at most supermarkets.

COPPA salted and dried sausage made from the neck or shoulder of pork. It is deep red in colour and is available mild and spicy; it is more marbled with fat so it's less expensive.

CORIANDER also known as cilantro or chinese parsley; bright-green-leafed herb with a pungent flavour. The stems and roots of coriander are also used in Thai cooking.

CORNICHON French for gherkin; a very small variety of pickled cucumber.

COS LETTUCE also known as romaine lettuce; the lettuce traditionally used in Caesar salad.

COUSCOUS a fine, grain-like cereal product from North Africa; made from semolina.

GLOSSARY

CURRY PASTES

green hottest of the traditional thai pastes; ingredients include green chilli, garlic, shallot, lemon grass, salt, galangal, shrimp paste, kaffir lime peel, coriander seed, pepper, cumin and turmeric. It is hotter than the milder *thai red curry paste*.

tandoori consists of garlic, ginger, tamarind, coriander, chilli and spices.

DIJON MUSTARD a pale brown, distinctively flavoured, fairly mild french mustard.

FLOUR

plain also known as all-purpose; unbleached wheat flour is the best for baking: the gluten content ensures a strong dough, which produces a light result.

self-raising all-purpose plain or wholemeal flour with baking powder and salt added; make yourself with plain or wholemeal flour sifted with baking powder in the proportion of 1 cup flour to 2 teaspoons baking powder.

GAI LAN also known as gai larn, chinese broccoli and chinese kale; a green vegetable appreciated more for its stems than its coarse leaves.

KAFFIR LIME LEAVES also known as bai magrood; look like two glossy dark green leaves joined end to end, forming a rounded hourglass shape. Sold fresh, dried or frozen, the dried leaves are less potent so double the number if using them as a substitute for fresh; a strip of fresh lime peel may be substituted for each kaffir lime leaf.

KUMARA Polynesian name of an orange-fleshed sweet potato often confused with yam.

LAMB BACKSTRAP also known as eye of loin; the larger fillet from a row of loin chops or cutlets. Tender and best cooked rapidly.

LEMON-FLAVOURED SPREAD commercially made lemon curd (a smooth spread, usually made from lemons, butter and eggs).

MAPLE SYRUP distilled from the sap of sugar maple trees. Maple-flavoured syrup or pancake syrup is not an adequate substitute for the real thing.

MESCLUN pronounced mess-kluhn; also known as mixed greens or spring salad mix. A commercial blend of assorted young lettuce and other green leaves, including baby spinach leaves, mizuna and curly endive.

MINCED MEAT also known as ground meat as in beef, veal, lamb, pork and chicken.

MIRIN a Japanese champagne-coloured cooking wine, made of glutinous rice and alcohol. It is used expressly for cooking and should not be confused with sake. A seasoned sweet mirin, manjo mirin, made of water, rice, corn syrup and alcohol, is used in various Japanese dipping sauces.

NOODLES

dried rice noodles also known as rice stick noodles. Made from rice flour and water, available flat and wide or very thin (*vermicelli*). Must be soaked in boiling water to soften.

fresh egg also called ba mee or yellow noodles; made from wheat flour and eggs, sold fresh or dried. Range in size from very fine strands to wide, spaghetti-like pieces as thick as a shoelace.

hokkien also known as stir-fry noodles. Fresh wheat flour noodles resembling thick, yellow-brown spaghetti; only require heating, not cooking.

soba thin japanese noodles made from a mix of buckwheat flour and wheat flour; available fresh or dried.

OIL

peanut pressed from ground peanuts; has a high smoke point (capacity to handle high heat without burning).

sesame produced from roasted crushed sesame seeds; a flavouring rather than a cooking medium.

PAPRIKA ground dried red capsicum; sold in sweet, smoked or hot flavours.

PEAS

snow also called mange tout (eat all); a variety of garden pea, eaten pod and all (although you may need to string them).

sugar snap also known as honey snap peas; fresh small pea that can be eaten whole, pod and all.

PEPITAS pale green kernels of dried pumpkin seeds; they can be bought plain or salted.

PEPPERONI spicy salami made of beef, pork and often veal.

PROSCIUTTO an unsmoked Italian ham that is salted, air-cured and aged. It is usually eaten uncooked.

RICE, WHITE LONG-GRAIN

elongated grains that remain separate when cooked; a popular steaming rice.

ROCKET also known as arugula, rugula and rucola; peppery green leaf eaten raw in salads or used in cooking. Baby rocket leaves are smaller and less peppery.

ROLLED OATS flattened oat grain rolled into flakes and traditionally used for porridge. Instant oats are also available, but use traditional oats for baking.

SAMBAL OELEK (also sambal ulek or olek); a salty paste made from ground chillies, garlic and vinegar.

SAUCES

black bean a Chinese sauce made from fermented soy beans, spices, water and wheat flour.

fish made from pulverised salted fermented fish (anchovies). Has a pungent smell and strong taste.

hoisin a thick, sweet and spicy Chinese barbecue sauce made from salted fermented soybeans, onions and garlic; used as a marinade or baste, or to accent stir-fries and barbecued or roasted foods. From Asian food shops and supermarkets.

kecap manis a dark, thick sweet soy sauce with molasses or palm sugar added when brewed.

light soy fairly thin in consistency and, while paler than the others, is the saltiest tasting; used in dishes in which the natural colour of the ingredients is to be maintained. Not to be confused with salt-reduced or low-sodium soy sauces.

oyster made from oysters and their brine, cooked with salt and soy sauce, and thickened with starches.

plum a thick, sweet and sour dipping sauce made from plums, vinegar, sugar, chillies and spices.

sweet chilli the comparatively mild Thai sauce made from red chillies, sugar, garlic and vinegar.

teriyaki either commercially bottled or home-made, this Japanese sauce, made from soy sauce, mirin, sugar, ginger and other spices, imparts a distinctive glaze when brushed over grilled meat or poultry. Teriyaki actually translates as lustrous (teri) grilled (yaki) food.

SOPRESSA a semi-hard pork salami typically flavoured with pepper, cloves, cinnamon, nutmeg, rosemary and garlic; has a delicate, slightly sweet, taste.

SUGAR

caster also known as superfine or finely granulated table sugar.

icing also known as confectioners' sugar or powdered sugar; pulverised granulated sugar crushed together with a small amount of cornflour.

palm also known as jaggery or gula melaka; made from the sap of the sugar palm tree. Light- to dark-brown in colour and usually sold in rock-hard cakes. Substitute dark brown sugar if you can't find palm sugar.

SUMAC a purple-red, astringent spice ground from berries growing on shrubs that flourish wild around the Mediterranean; adds a tart, lemony flavour to dips and dressings and goes well with barbecued meat.

TOMATOES

egg also called plum or roma; these are smallish, oval-shaped tomatoes.

VANILLA EXTRACT obtained from vanilla beans infused in water; a non-alcoholic version of essence.

VERMICELLI see noodles, dried rice.

VINEGAR

apple cider made from fermented apples. Available from supermarkets and health food stores.

balsamic originally from Modena, Italy, there are now many balsamic vinegars on the market ranging in pungency and quality depending on how, and how long, they have been aged. Quality can be determined up to a point by price; use the most expensive sparingly.

red wine made from red wine.

WATER CHESTNUTS resemble true chestnuts in appearance, hence the English name. Small brown tubers with a crisp, white, nutty-tasting flesh. Their crunchy texture is best experienced fresh; however, canned water chestnuts are more easily obtained and can be kept for about a month in the fridge, once opened. Used, rinsed and drained, in salads and stir-fries.

WATERCRESS one of the cress family, a large group of peppery greens. Highly perishable, so must be used as soon as possible after purchase.

WITLOF also known as belgian endive; related to and confused with chicory.

WOMBOK also known as chinese cabbage; elongated with pale green crinkly leaves, is the most commonly used cabbage in South-East Asia.

ZA'ATAR dry blend of roasted sesame seeds, wild marjoram, thyme and sumac; available in Arabic specialty shops.

ZUCCHINI also known as courgette; belongs to the squash family. Yellow flowers can be stuffed or used in salads.

CONVERSION CHART

MEASURES

One Australian metric measuring cup holds approximately 250ml, one Australian metric tablespoon holds 20ml, one Australian metric teaspoon holds 5ml.

The difference between one country's measuring cups and another's is within a 2- or 3-teaspoon variance, and will not affect your cooking results. North America, New Zealand and the United Kingdom use a 15ml tablespoon. All cup and spoon measurements are level. The most accurate way of measuring dry ingredients is to weigh them. When measuring liquids, use a clear glass or plastic jug with metric markings.

We use large eggs with an average weight of 60g.

DRY MEASURES

METRIC	IMPERIAL
15g	½oz
30g	1oz
60g	2oz
90g	3oz
125g	4oz (¼lb)
155g	5oz
185g	6oz
220g	7oz
250g	8oz (½lb)
280g	9oz
315g	10oz
345g	11oz
375g	12oz (¾lb)
410g	13oz
440g	14oz
470g	15oz
500g	16oz (1lb)
750g	24oz (1½lb)
1kg	32oz (2lb)

LIQUID MEASURES

METRIC	IMPERIAL
30ml	1 fluid oz
60ml	2 fluid oz
100ml	3 fluid oz
125ml	4 fluid oz
150ml	5 fluid oz
190ml	6 fluid oz
250ml	8 fluid oz
300ml	10 fluid oz
500ml	16 fluid oz
600ml	20 fluid oz
1000ml (1 litre)	1¾ pints

LENGTH MEASURES

METRIC	IMPERIAL
3mm	⅛in
6mm	¼in
1cm	½in
2cm	¾in
2.5cm	1in
5cm	2in
6cm	2½in
8cm	3in
10cm	4in
13cm	5in
15cm	6in
18cm	7in
20cm	8in
23cm	9in
25cm	10in
28cm	11in
30cm	12in (1ft)

OVEN TEMPERATURES

These oven temperatures are only a guide for conventional ovens.
For fan-forced ovens, check the manufacturer's manual.

	°C (CELSIUS)	°F (FAHRENHEIT)
Very slow	120	250
Slow	150	275-300
Moderately slow	160	325
Moderate	180	350-375
Moderately hot	200	400
Hot	220	425-450
Very hot	240	475

The imperial measurements used in these recipes are approximate only and should not affect your cooking results.

INDEX

First Published in 2011 by ACP Magazines Ltd,
a division of PBL Media Pty Limited
54 Park St, Sydney
GPO Box 4088, Sydney, NSW 2001.
phone (02) 9282 8618; fax (02) 9267 9438
acpbooks@acpmagazines.com.au; www.acpbooks.com.au

ACP BOOKS
General Manager · Christine Whiston
Associate publisher · Seymour Cohen
Editor-in-Chief · Susan Tomnay
Creative Director · Hieu Chi Nguyen
Food Director · Pamela Clark

Published and Distributed in the United Kingdom by Octopus Publishing Group
Endeavour House
189 Shaftesbury Avenue
London WC2H 8JY
United Kingdom
phone (+44)(0)207 632 5400; fax (+44)(0)207 632 5405
info@octopus-publishing.co.uk;
www.octopusbooks.co.uk

Printed by Toppan Printing Co., China

International foreign language rights, Brian Cearnes, ACP Books bcearnes@acpmagazines.com.au

A catalogue record for this book is available from the British Library.
ISBN 9781742450612